ANIMALS
That Make a Difference!

Dogs

Ashley Lee

Explore other books at:
WWW.ENGAGEBOOKS.COM

VANCOUVER, B.C.

e↗ WWW.ENGAGEBOOKS.COM

Dogs: Level 2
Animals That Make a Difference!
Lee, Ashley 1995 –
Text © 2020 Engage Books
Design © 2020 Engage Books

Edited by: A.R. Roumanis,
Jared Siemens, and Lauren Dick
Design by: A.R. Roumanis

Text set in Arial Regular.
Chapter headings set in Arial Black.

FIRST EDITION / FIRST PRINTING

LIBRARY AND ARCHIVES CANADA CATALOGUING IN PUBLICATION

Title: Dogs: Animals That Make a Difference Level 2 reader / Ashley Lee
Names: Lee, Ashley, 1995- author

Identifiers: Canadiana (print) 20200308874 | Canadiana (ebook) 20200308912
ISBN 978-1-77437-612-6 (hardcover)
ISBN 978-1-77437-611-9 (softcover)
ISBN 978-1-77437-613-3 (pdf)
ISBN 978-1-77437-614-0 (epub)
ISBN 978-1-77437-615-7 (kindle)

Subjects:
LCSH: Dogs—Juvenile literature
LCSH: Working dogs—Juvenile literature
LCSH: Human-animal relationships—Juvenile literature

Classification: SF426.5 .L44 20200 | DDC J636.7—DC23

Contents

What Are Dogs?

Dogs are **mammals**. They are related to wolves. Dogs have been trained to live with people.

KEY WORD

Mammals: animals with warm blood and bones in their backs.

Dogs are one of the most common animals kept by people. They are very helpful to people, other animals, and Earth.

A Closer Look

Dogs who look the same are part of groups called breeds. The smallest dog breeds are only about 5 inches (13 centimeters) tall. Large dog breeds can be up to 30 inches (76 cm) high.

Most dogs have tails that help them keep their balance.

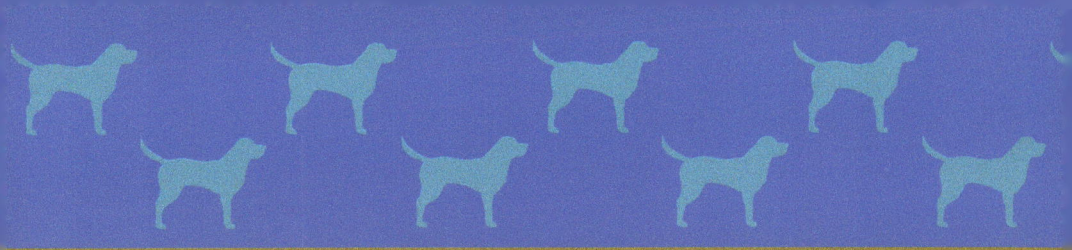

Dogs have sharp teeth. The long pointed teeth are called canines. They are used to tear food apart.

Dogs have five toes on each foot with claws on the ends.

Where Do Dogs Live?

Dogs are related to the gray wolf. Dogs were first found in Europe or Asia more than 15,000 year ago! Today, dogs live all over the world.

The husky is a sled dog that was raised in Siberia. Chilean terriers were the first dog breed to come from Chile. Boerboels are farm dogs that come from South Africa.

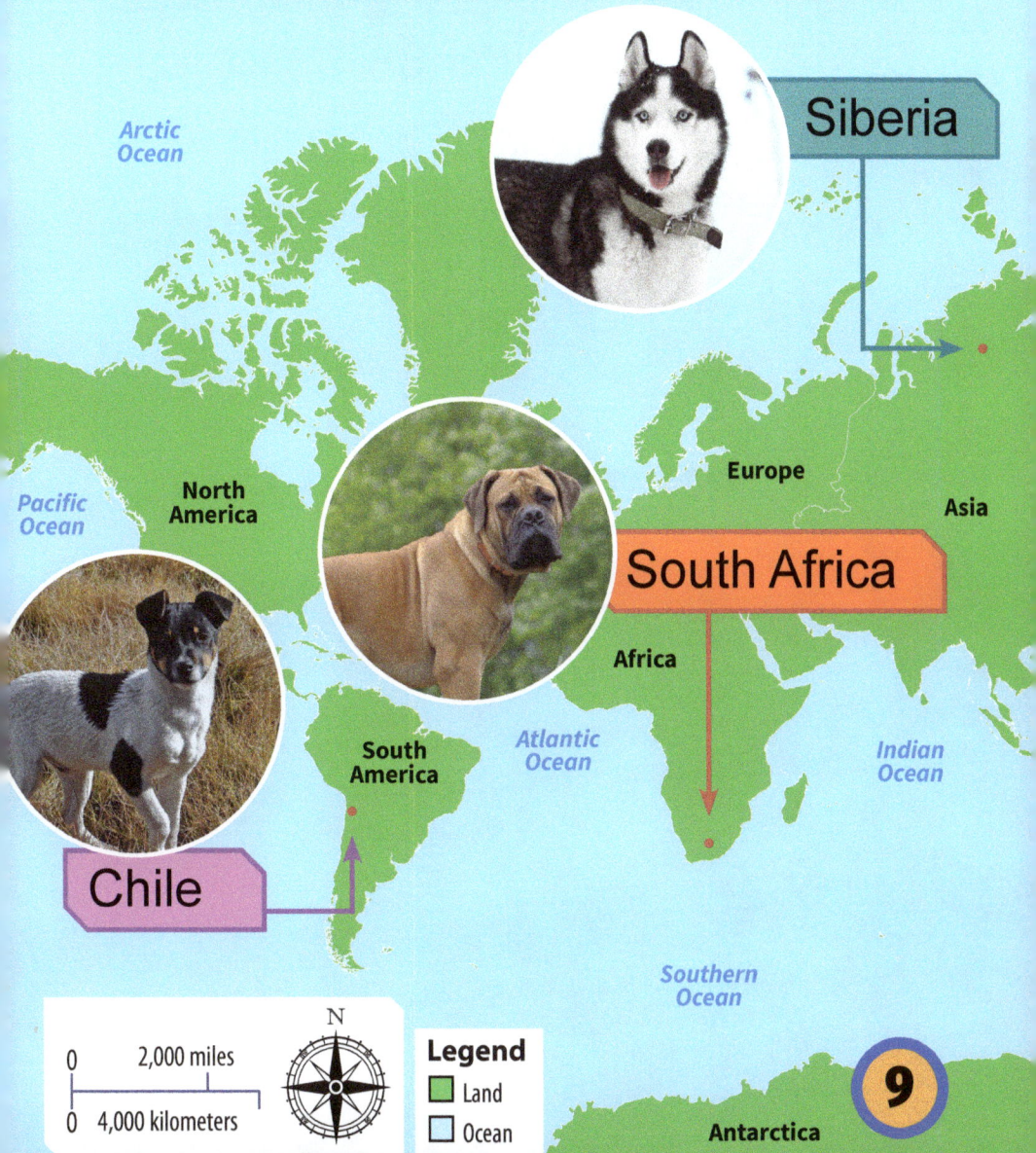

Arctic Ocean

Siberia

North America

Pacific Ocean

Europe

Asia

South Africa

Africa

South America

Atlantic Ocean

Indian Ocean

Chile

Southern Ocean

0 — 2,000 miles

0 — 4,000 kilometers

N

Legend
- Land
- Ocean

Antarctica

What Do Dogs Eat?

Dogs mostly eat meat. Many dogs eat fish like salmon or tuna. Beef, chicken, and pork are the most common foods for dogs.

Many dogs eat dry food called kibble. Kibble is a mix of dried meat, vegetables, and grains.

Some dogs eat raw food diets. This means they eat meat and vegetables that have not been cooked.

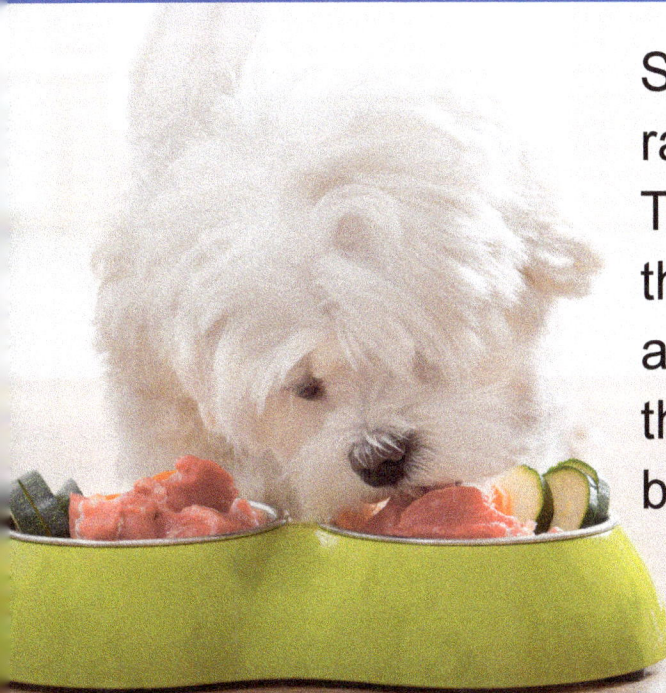

How Do Dogs Talk to Each Other?

Dogs talk to each other and people by barking, howling, or whining. They will also move their bodies to show how they feel.

Dogs bark to get attention, to warn others of danger, or when they are excited.

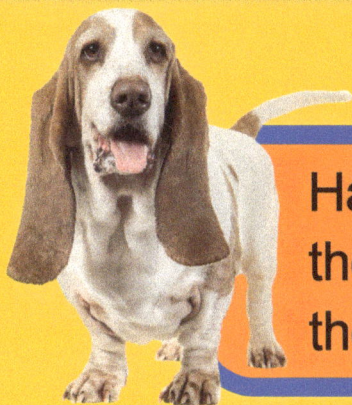

Happy dogs will wag their tails and hang their mouths open.

Dogs who are scared may whine and show their teeth. They will also tuck their tail under their body.

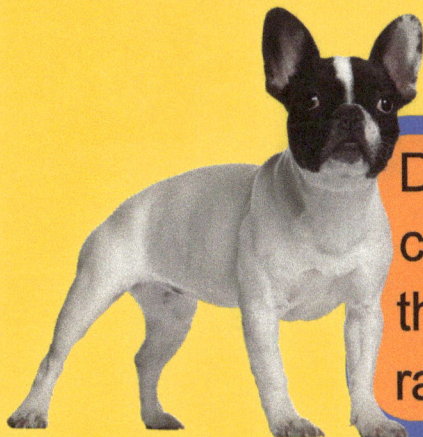

Dogs who are curious will stiffen their bodies and raise their ears.

Dog Life Cycle

Baby dogs are called puppies. Puppies' eyes stay closed until they are about 2 weeks old. Puppies start to become adults between 6 and 18 months.

Adult dogs become seniors between 6 and 10 years old. Senior dogs often need extra care. Very big dogs live to be 7 or 8 years old. Small dogs can live for more than 15 years.

Curious Facts About Dogs

More people own Labrador retrievers than any other kind of dog.

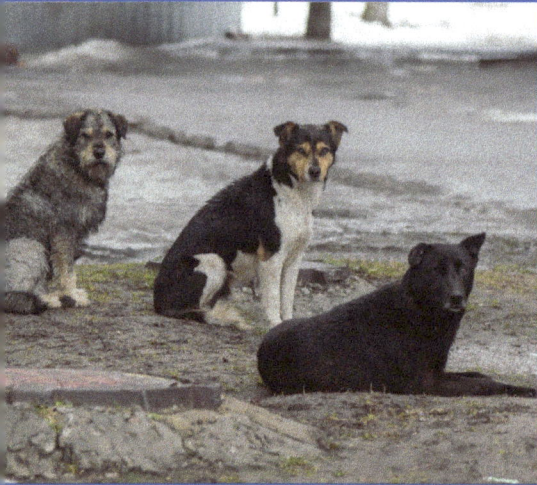

Some dogs do not live with people. They are called stray or feral dogs. These dogs live together in groups called packs.

Dogs dream, just like humans.

Every dog's nose print is unique, just like human fingerprints.

One of the world's oldest dog breeds is the Saluki.

There are around 600 million dogs in the world.

Kinds of Dogs

Sporting dogs like retrievers are used for hunting birds. They fetch birds from water.

Hound dogs like beagles are also used for hunting. They have a strong sense of smell.

Terriers like Boston terriers are used for protecting homes. They chase away small animals like rats.

Herding dogs like border collies gather and protect farm animals.

Working dogs like Great Danes are used to protect people.

Toy dogs like Chihuahuas are small dogs used to keep people company.

Non-sporting dogs like poodles are dogs that do not fit into any other group.

How Dogs Help Other Animals

Some dogs have been trained to find animals that are in danger of disappearing forever. These dogs are called conservation dogs.

Conservation dogs use their strong sense of smell to find animals in danger and bring people to help keep them safe.

Dogs in Iowa have been trained to find rare turtles. When a dog finds a turtle, they gently pick it up with their mouth and take it to a person to be protected.

How Dogs Help Earth

Dogs use their strong sense of smell to help humans find plants that hurt other plants. Plants that harm other plants are called invasive species.

When dogs find invasive species, people are able to remove them to help other plants grow.

How Dogs Help Humans

Trained dogs called service dogs help people with disabilities. Some service dogs help guide people who cannot see.

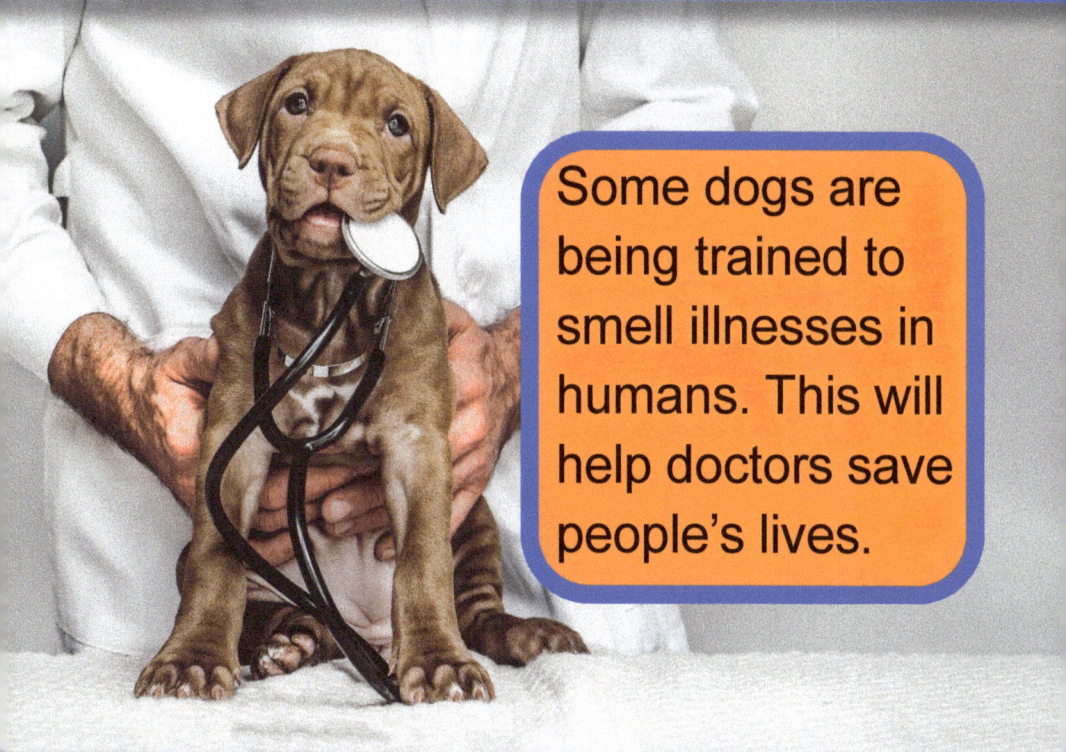

Some dogs are being trained to smell illnesses in humans. This will help doctors save people's lives.

Search and Rescue dogs use their sense of smell to help find people who are lost or in danger.

Dogs in Danger

Some dog breeds have gone extinct. This means there are no more left in the world. Some breeds are in danger of going extinct. They are called endangered species.

Otterhounds were once used to hunt otters. When otter hunting became illegal, otterhounds became less popular.

Irish water spaniels are used to fetch birds for hunters. Some similar breeds are already extinct.

Queen Victoria had a Skye terrier about 200 years ago. This made them a popular breed at the time. Their numbers have since gone down.

How To Help Dogs

Many animal shelters are full, which means they cannot take in any more dogs. Adopting a dog from a shelter frees up space so the shelter can help another dog in need.

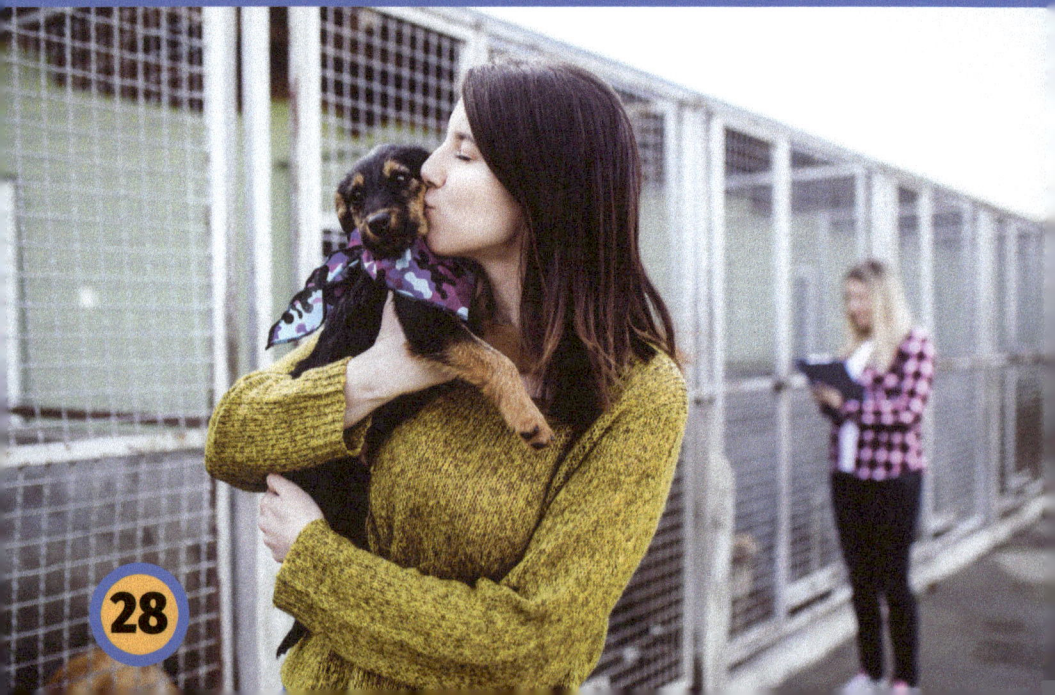

Animal shelters are always in need of donations and welcome second-hand supplies. Shelters can use old blankets, towels, cleaning supplies, or used leashes.

Dog shelters need volunteers to help take dogs for regular walks.

Quiz

Test your knowledge of dogs by answering the following questions. The questions are based on what you have read in this book. The answers are listed on the bottom of the next page.

1 What animal are dogs related to?

2 What do dogs eat?

3 How do dogs talk to each other?

4 At what age do dogs become adults?

5 What kind of dogs gather and protect farm animals?

6 What are dogs who help people with disabilities called?

Explore other books in the Animals That Make a Difference series.

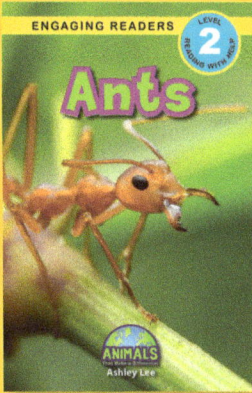

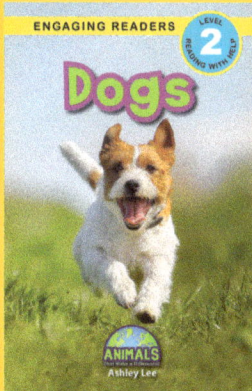

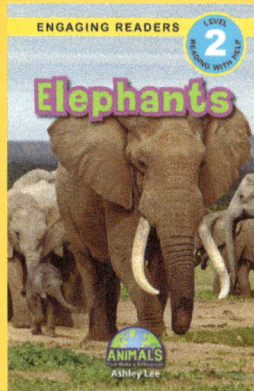

Ants — ENGAGING READERS — LEVEL 2

Beavers — ENGAGING READERS — LEVEL 2

Butterflies — ENGAGING READERS — LEVEL 2

Dogs — ENGAGING READERS — LEVEL 2

Elephants — ENGAGING READERS — LEVEL 2

Frogs — ENGAGING READERS — LEVEL 2

Llamas — ENGAGING READERS — LEVEL 2

Octopuses — ENGAGING READERS — LEVEL 2

Primates — ENGAGING READERS — LEVEL 2

Visit www.engagebooks.com to explore more Engaging Readers.